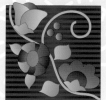

Super Simple Strips

Nancy Smith and Lynda Milligan

Credits

Sharon Holmes – Editor, Technical Illustrator
Susan Johnson – Cover, Graphics, Quilt Design, Photo Stylist
Lexie Foster – Cover, Graphics, Quilt Design, Photo Stylist
Christine Scott – Editorial Assistant
Sandi Fruehling – Copy Reader
Brad Bartholomew – Photographer

Thanks

Sewing & Machine Quilting – Ann Petersen, Jane Dumler, Katie Wells,
Courtenay Hughes, Susan Auskaps, Sue Williams, Barbara Karst
Long-arm Machine Quilting – Sandi Fruehling, Susan F. Geddes,
Kay Morrison, Carolyn Schmitt, Suzanne Michelle Hyland
Selected props from the home of Susan and Bob Julian

POSSIBILITIES®

…Fabric designers for AvLyn Inc., publishers of DreamSpinners®
patterns & I'll Teach Myself® & Possibilities® books…
Home of Great American Quilt Factory, Inc.

Super Simple Strips   ©2003 Nancy Smith & Lynda Milligan

Published in the United States of America by Possibilities®, Denver, Colorado
ISBN: 1-880972-52-2

MAKE MORE QUILTS

Fabric lovers of the world–here is another chance for you to **make more quilts**! This book is a sequel to *Super Simple Squares*, a book in which all of the quilts were constructed with 6½" squares. In *Super Simple Strips*, all the quilts are constructed with 6½" strips. Check your local quilt shop for beautifully bundled collections of 6½" strips. In our shop we make these with 20 fabrics–perfect for any quilt in this book.

If precut collections are not available, use the delightful combinations below as inspiration for choosing just the right fabrics for your quilt. Yardage requirements are also given for buying fabric off the bolt.

One way we choose fabric is by starting with a colorful print and then gathering fabrics that coordinate. The colorful print might then become the perfect border.

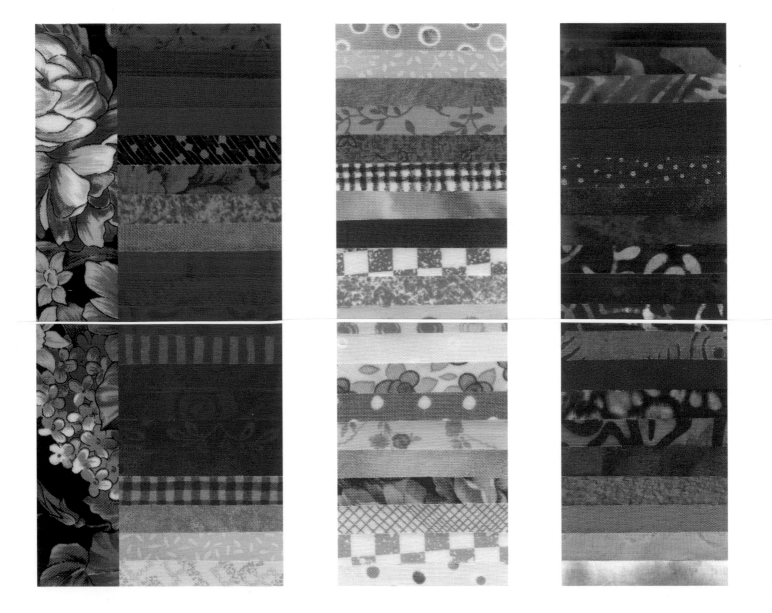

GENERAL DIRECTIONS

FABRIC PREPARATION

One-hundred percent cotton fabrics 42–44" wide are recommended for quilting. Our yardage is based on this width, including a bit for shrinkage during washing. Washing and tumble drying quilting fabric has the advantage of maximizing the shrinkage and removing excess dye. Unwashed fabric retains its crispness and body, making it very easy to use, but the quilter must assume the risk of shrinkage and color bleeding. When using washed fabric, spray sizing or lightweight starch can be used to restore body.

We do not recommend prewashing fabric from rolls.

ROTARY CUTTING

A transparent rotary cutting ruler, a rotary cutter with a sharp blade, and a self-healing rotary-cutting mat are needed. Unless otherwise indicated, cuts should be made from selvage to selvage. Reverse directions if you are left handed.

1. Fold the fabric in half with the selvage edges even. Slide the selvages back and forth until there is no twist in the fabric, then lay it on the mat with the selvage edges toward you. Fold the fabric in half again, matching the selvage edges with the folded edge. It is important that these folds are straight, or the strips will be bowed. There are now four thicknesses of fabric.

2. Using a transparent rotary cutting ruler, match up a line on the ruler with the fold of the fabric. Make sure that the right edge of the ruler covers all four layers.

3. Trim off the excess fabric by holding the rotary cutting blade flat against the right edge of the ruler and place it just off the edge of fabric closest to you. To stabilize the ruler, place your hand so that two fingers extend off the left side of the ruler onto the fabric. Push the rotary cutter away from you to cut off the right edge of fabric. The result is a straight edge from which to begin cutting strips.

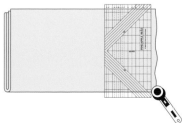

4. Swing mat and fabric around 180°.

5. Position ruler so marking for desired strip width is even with just-cut edges of fabric. Keep top and bottom edges of fabric parallel to horizontal lines of ruler.

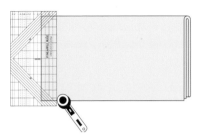

6. Cut away from you, then move strip carefully away from folded fabric to assist in placement of ruler for next cut.

7. If many squares of the same size are needed, cut a strip the size of the square and then crosscut the strip into squares.

8. For half-square and quarter-square triangles, cut squares the size listed in the directions for each quilt and then line the ruler up from corner to corner and cut the square into triangles.

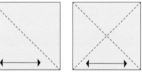

FUSIBLE WEB APPLIQUE

1. Trace patterns the reverse of the direction wanted onto smooth, paper side of fusible web. Cut shapes apart ⅛-¼" outside traced lines. For large shapes, cut out the center, leaving just a margin of web. Note: Patterns in this book have already been reversed for tracing.

2. Avoiding selvage, press rough side of fusible web to wrong side of fabric. Cut out shapes on traced lines.

3. Peel off paper. Position applique on background fabric and fuse in place. If design is layered, arrange all appliques before fusing. A great tool for building layered appliques before applying them to a background is an applique pressing sheet.

4. SATIN STITCH: Place tear-away stabilizer under background fabric. Use a very short stitch length and a medium zigzag stitch width. Loosen top tension

as needed to keep bobbin thread from showing on top of work. Keep threads of satin stitch at right angles to edge of applique by pivoting as needed. To make tapered points, reduce stitch width while sewing. To tie off threads, bring stitch width to zero, slide fabric to left or right, and take 6-8 stitches next to satin stitching. Tear away the stabilizer.

INVISIBLE OPEN ZIGZAG: This is a fast way to secure edges of fused appliques without creating an outline of thread as in satin stitch. Use a narrow stitch width and a medium-short stitch length to create a small, open zigzag. Use nylon monofilament thread as the top thread only.

MACHINE BLANKET STITCH: Some machines have a squared-off zigzag stitch called a blanket or buttonhole stitch (not the settings used for garment buttonholes, but a decorative stitch). Refer to individual sewing machine manuals for directions. No stabilizer is needed behind the background fabric. Many threads can be used for this stitch, each creating a different look. Jeans thread used with a large machine blanket stitch setting looks just like hand buttonhole stitching. Try experimenting with other decorative machine stitches.

PIECING & PRESSING

1. Establish a ¼″ seam allowance on your sewing machine. If the machine does not have a quarter-inch presser foot or adjustable needle positions, place a rotary cutting ruler under the sewing machine needle. Line up the ruler with the first ¼″ line directly under the needle. Lower the needle carefully. Make sure the ruler is square to the front of the machine. Place a piece of masking tape along the edge of the ruler on the throat plate and use it as a guide for the edge of your fabric.

2. Use a light neutral cotton thread when sewing most fabrics. If all fabrics are dark, use a dark thread. Thread in the top and bobbin should be the same type to make the most consistent stitches.

3. Place the pieces to be joined right sides together. Pin, matching seam lines, and sew, using an accurate ¼″ seam allowance and a straight stitch, 10-12 stitches per inch. A short stitch length will make it unnecessary to backstitch at the beginning and end of seams. Press seam allowances to one side, usually toward the darker

fabric unless otherwise noted. If you have trouble with loose threads at the beginning of a seam or with the points of a triangle being pushed down into the throat plate, start sewing on a folded fabric scrap and then feed the pieces under the presser foot.

4. Use an iron set for cotton and an up-and-down motion rather than a pushing motion. The goal is to set the seams and remove wrinkles without distortion. With the dark fabric on top, press the pieces flat, as they were sewn, to set the stitches. Then, without moving the fabric, fold the top fabric over the stitching line and press the seam. This works well for long strips as well as small pieces.

PIECING TIPS

Chain piecing saves time and thread. After sewing a seam, immediately feed in a new set of pieces without lifting the presser foot or clipping threads. Sew as many sets as possible in this manner, and then clip them apart. With long strips, take care not to pull or stretch the strips, or they may become wavy.

Where two seams meet, position one seam allowance in one direction and one seam allowance in the opposite direction. Push the seams together tightly; they will hold each other in place, making it unnecessary to pin.

When crossing seam intersections of triangles, aim for spot where seam lines intersect to avoid cutting off points in patchwork.

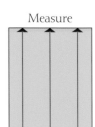

If one edge appears to be larger, put that side next to the feed-dog so excess will be eased into seam without leaving tucks.

ADDING BORDERS

Most of the borders in this book are stitched on sides first and then top and bottom.

1. To determine the length of the side borders, measure the length of the quilt from cut edge to cut edge in at least three places. Average these measurements.

   Measure

   Note: Do not measure along the edges since edges are often stretched and can therefore be longer.

2. Stitch crossgrain (selvage-to-selvage) cuts of fabric end to end to equal the average length of the quilt top.

3. Fold one side border and one side of quilt top into quarters and mark with pins. Matching marked points, pin border to quilt, right sides together. This distributes any ease along the entire edge of the quilt.

Mark, match, & stitch

4. Stitch border to quilt. If one edge is slightly longer, put that side against the feed-dog, and the excess will be eased into the seam. Repeat for other side of quilt.

5. Repeat measuring and stitching process for top and bottom borders of quilt.

6. For a second or third border, measure down the center of the previous border. Stitch the side borders to the quilt, then measure for top and bottom borders.

7. Press border seams toward outside edge of quilt.

MACHINE QUILTING

A quilt is much easier to mark before it is layered. There are a number of good quality marking pens and pencils available. Experiment with several to find one that is easy to use and is removable. Select a quilting design and mark the top lightly.

For quilts that require pieced backings, piece the backing either horizontally or vertically (directions for each quilt include this information). Allow at least 2" to extend beyond the quilt top. Basting joins the three layers together in preparation for quilting. All of the quilts in this book have been machine quilted.

Safety pinning or spray basting works well for machine quilting. For safety pin basting, use one-inch safety pins placed four to six inches apart in spots where they will not be in the way of planned quilting lines. If spray basting, lightly spray the wrong side of the backing fabric and anchor it flat to the floor—either by taping to a hard floor or pinning into the carpet. Place the batting on the backing and smooth it out. Then lightly spray the wrong side of the quilt top, center it on the batting, and smooth it. Release backing from floor, turn quilt over, and work out any wrinkles on the back.

For straight-line machine quilting, use an even-feed or walking foot. For free-motion quilting, use a darning or quilting foot and lower or cover the feed-dog. If you haven't machine quilted before, it is wise to stitch a practice piece first. Let your experience and preferences guide you in determining how to quilt each project. Machine quilting takes practice, and a class at a local quilt store is a good investment.

BINDING

1. Trim batting and backing even with quilt top.

2. Cut 2½" strips on the crossgrain of the fabric. Stitch end to end to fit all the way around the quilt.

3. Press binding in half lengthwise, wrong sides together. Leaving an 8" tail of binding and using a ⅜" seam allowance, begin stitching binding to right side of quilt at least 12" from one of the corners. Stop stitching at seam intersection of first corner. Leave needle in fabric, pivot, and stitch off corner of quilt.

4. Pull quilt slightly away from machine, leaving threads attached. Make a 45° fold in binding.

5. Fold again, placing second fold even with top edge of quilt and raw edges of binding even with right raw edge of quilt.

6. Resume stitching at top edge using a ⅜" seam allowance.

7. After making all four mitered corners, stop stitching 10" from where you started. Take quilt out of machine. Lay ends of binding along unstitched edge of quilt. Trim ends so they overlap by ½".

8. Unfold binding and pull ends away from quilt. Place ends of binding right sides together, stitch with ¼" seam, and finger press seam open. Refold binding and place it along unstitched edge of quilt. Stitch remaining section of binding to quilt.

9. Turn binding to back and hand stitch folded edge to cover stitched line. To distribute bulk, fold each corner miter in the opposite direction from which it was folded and stitched on the front.

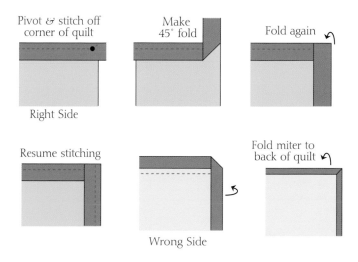

Pivot & stitch off corner of quilt

Make 45° fold

Fold again

Right Side

Resume stitching

Wrong Side

Fold miter to back of quilt

Approximately 40 x 48″

YARDAGE Choose fabric with 42″ usable width.

DOUBLE YOUR FUN! YARDAGE MAKES 2 QUILTS:

Novelty stripe	1¼ yd
Coordinating prints	¼ yd each of 20 fabrics
	OR 1 roll of 20 strips 6½″ wide
Binding	1 yd
Backing	4¼ yd
Batting	2 pieces 46 x 54″

CUTTING *Cut these strips from selvage to selvage.

Stripe	3–4 pieces for each quilt – cut along motif lines adding ¼″ seam allowance on each side – 42″ long by various widths
Prints	*7–15 pieces for each quilt – 1½–6″ wide
Binding	*5 strips 2½″ wide for each quilt

DIRECTIONS Use ¼″ seam allowance unless otherwise noted.

1. QUILT TOPS: Remove selvages from ends of strips. Cut all strips to the same length as the shortest one. Trim strips cut from novelty stripe to same length. Place all strips on floor or design wall and change their positions as desired. If quilt is too long, adjust length by eliminating a print strip or cutting a few of the print strips to narrower widths. Stitch strips together. Press.

2. LAYER, QUILT, & BIND: Cut 3 pieces of backing 46″ long. Piece together along 46″ sides. Cut 2 backings 46 x 54″. See Machine Quilting and Binding, page 5.

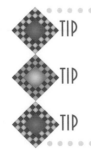

TIP

TIP

TIP

Make a design wall by covering an insulation foam board with cotton batting, needlepunch, or heavy flannel. Attach to wall, or leave unattached so it can be moved around your sewing room.

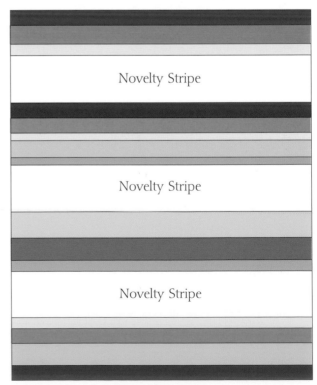

Example Layout

Example Layout

STUDY IN BLUE

STUDY IN BLUE

Approximately 62 x 81"

YARDAGE Choose fabric with 42" usable width.

Coordinating prints	¼ yd each of 20 fabrics OR 1 roll of 20 strips 6½" wide
Sashing	2⅜ yd
Binding	⅔ yd
Backing	5¼ yd
Batting	68 x 87"

CUTTING *Cut these strips from selvage to selvage.

Prints	Cut 14 of the 6½" strips or quarter yards as shown in diagram at right
	Cut 2-3 squares 6½" from each of the remaining 6 strips for prairie points
Sashing	10 strips 3" wide on lengthwise grain
Binding	*8 strips 2½" wide

DIRECTIONS Use ¼" seam allowance unless otherwise noted.

1. ROWS: Place pieces on floor or design wall in vertical rows using 2 pieces of each size for each row. Rearrange as desired. Stitch pieces into rows. Press.

2. PRAIRIE POINTS: Press squares in half diagonally, wrong sides together. Press in half diagonally again. Place prairie points on vertical rows in groups of 2 or 3 using diagram and photo as a guide. Side one into the folds of the next one to overlap them. Pin or baste in place, matching raw edges of prairie points with raw edges of pieced rows.

3. ASSEMBLY: Cut 8 strips of sashing to same length as rows. Stitch sashing and rows together as shown. Press. Cut 2 strips of sashing to same width as quilt. Stitch to quilt. Press.

4. LAYER, QUILT, & BIND: Piece backing vertically to same size as batting. See Machine Quilting and Binding, page 5.

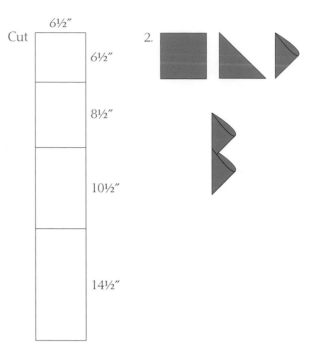

Cut 6½" — 6½" — 8½" — 10½" — 14½"

2.

2-3.

TIP

TIP

TIP

The large prairie points can be held down in a variety of ways after the quilting is complete: tack the point down invisibly with thread, sew a button near the tip, or use yarn or embroidery floss to make a decorative "tie".

56 x 66"

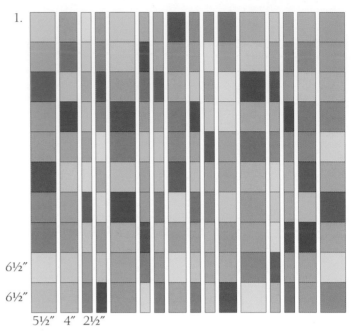

1.

YARDAGE Choose fabric with 42" usable width.

Quilt center	¼ yd each of 20 fabrics
	OR 1 roll of 20 strips 6½" wide
Border	¼ yd each of 4 fabrics
Binding	⅜ yd each of 2 fabrics
Backing	3¾ yd
Batting	62 x 72"

CUTTING *Cut these strips from selvage to selvage.

Quilt center	Cut each 6½" strip or quarter yard as shown in diagram at right
Border	*2 strips 3½" wide from each fabric
Binding	*4 strips 2½" wide from each fabric

DIRECTIONS Use ¼" seam allowance unless otherwise noted.

1. CENTER: Placing fabrics randomly, stitch 4 vertical rows of ten 5½" pieces, 4 vertical rows of ten 4" pieces, and 8 vertical rows of ten 2½" pieces. See diagram. Place rows on floor and flip them from top to bottom as needed to evenly distribute fabrics and color throughout quilt. Stitch rows together. Press.

2. BORDER: Stitch the 2 border strips of each fabric together. Choose 2 fabrics for sides of quilt–trim to same length as quilt. See diagram. Stitch to sides. Repeat at top and bottom. Press.

3. LAYER, QUILT, & BIND: Piece backing horizontally to same size as batting. See Machine Quilting and Binding, page 5. Bind top and bottom of quilt with one binding fabric and sides with the other fabric.

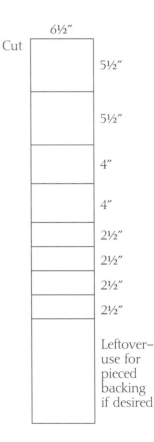

6½" 5½" / 4" / 2½" (6½" label at left; 5½", 4", 2½" labels at bottom)

Cut — 6½"

5½"
5½"
4"
4"
2½"
2½"
2½"
2½"
Leftover– use for pieced backing if desired

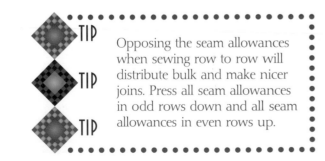

TIP
TIP
TIP

Opposing the seam allowances when sewing row to row will distribute bulk and make nicer joins. Press all seam allowances in odd rows down and all seam allowances in even rows up.

56x66"

2–3.

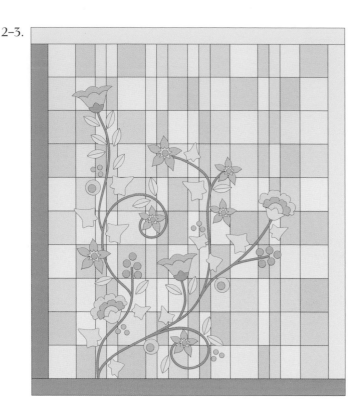

YARDAGE Choose fabric with 42" usable width.

Quilt center	¼ yd each of 20 fabrics
	OR 1 roll of 20 strips 6½" wide
Applique	⅛ yd each of 9 or more fabrics for flowers
	⅙ yd each of 2 or more fabrics for leaves
	½ yd for bias-cut vine & leaves
Border	½ yd each of 2 fabrics
Binding	⅝ yd
Backing	3¾ yd
Batting	62x72"

CUTTING *Cut these strips from selvage to selvage.

Quilt center	Cut each 6½" strip or quarter yard as shown in diagram at right
Applique	See Step 2, patterns on pages 45–46
Border	*4 strips 3½" wide from each fabric
Binding	*7 strips 2½" wide

DIRECTIONS Use ¼" seam allowance unless otherwise noted.

1. CENTER: See Step 1 and diagram on page 10.

2. APPLIQUE: Cut 12 bias strips 20" long and ¼–⅜" wide from vine/leaf fabric bonded with fusible web. Using photo and diagram as guides for placement, arrange appliques using flowers or leaves to cover raw edges where vine segments join. See Fusible Web Applique, page 3, and Tip box below.

3. BORDER: Stitch 2 border strips of each fabric together and trim to same length as quilt. See diagram. Stitch to sides. Repeat at top and bottom. Press.

4. LAYER, QUILT, & BIND: Piece backing horizontally to same size as batting. See Machine Quilting and Binding, page 5.

TIP

TIP

TIP

When preparing the fabric for the small leaves, stitch two strips together before bonding with fusible web. The seam becomes the center line of the leaf.

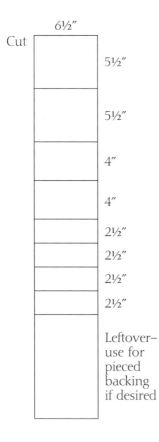

6½"

Cut

5½"

5½"

4"

4"

2½"

2½"

2½"

2½"

Leftover– use for pieced backing if desired

PERSIAN BEAUTY

56 x 70"

YARDAGE Choose fabric with 42" usable width.

Quilt center, applique   ¼ yd each of 20 fabrics
                          OR 1 roll of 20 strips 6½" wide

Applique
  Vine, leaves   ½ yd
  Optional: Larger
    flowers & leaves   ⅛ yd each of additional fabrics as desired
Border   1¾ yd
Binding   ⅝ yd
Backing   3¾ yd
Batting   62 x 76"

CUTTING *Cut these strips from selvage to selvage.

Applique   Set aside 4 of the 20 fabrics to use for
               applique. Also use leftover pieces from
               Step 1. Patterns on page 44.

Quilt center   Cut from each of 5 fabrics:
                 *3 strips 1½" wide
               Cut from each of 4 fabrics:
                 *3 strips 2" wide
               Cut from each of 3 fabrics:
                 *2 strips 2½" wide
               Cut from each of 4 fabrics:
                 *2 strips 3" wide
Border   4 strips 8½" wide on lengthwise grain
Binding   *7 strips 2½" wide

DIRECTIONS Use ¼" seam allowance unless otherwise noted.

1. CENTER: Remove selvages from ends of strips. Cut all strips
   to the same length as the shortest one. Place strips on floor
   or design wall and change their positions as desired. Center
   should measure approximately 40 x 54". Use leftover pieces
   for applique. Stitch strips together in sets of 4–6. Stitch sets
   together. Press.

2. BORDER: See Adding Borders, page 4.

3. APPLIQUE: Cut 8 bias strips 20" long and ¼-⅜" wide from
   vine/leaf fabric bonded with fusible web. Using photo and
   diagram as guides for placement, arrange appliques. See
   Fusible Web Applique, page 3.

4. LAYER, QUILT, & BIND: Piece backing horizontally to same
   size as batting. See Machine Quilting and Binding, page 5.

1.

2-3.

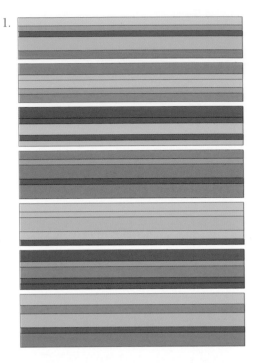

62 x 68"

YARDAGE Choose fabric with 42" usable width.

Quilt center,

Border 2	¼ yd each of 20 fabrics
	OR 1 roll of 20 strips 6½" wide
Border 1	⅝ yd
Border 3	¾ yd
Binding	⅝ yd
Backing	4 yd
Batting	68 x 74"

CUTTING *Cut these strips from selvage to selvage.

Quilt center, Border 2	Cut from each fabric:
	*2 strips 3" wide
Border 1	*6 strips 3" wide
Border 3	*7 strips 3" wide
Binding	*7 strips 2½" wide

DIRECTIONS Use ¼" seam allowance unless otherwise noted.

1. CENTER & BORDER 2:

   a. Using a rotary cutter, trim selvages from ends of strips with a careful 90° cut. Cut each strip, with a careful 90° cut, into 4 pieces: 6½", 8½", 10½", and 14½" long.

   b. Stitch all strips together end to end in random order using a diagonal seam: press 45° angle on end of strip to be placed on top each time, stitch on fold, and *do not trim* triangles at this time. Press all seam allowances in the same direction. See diagrams.

   c. Trim each seam with a rotary cutter and ruler, leaving ¼" seam allowance. Set pairs of triangles aside carefully so they can be picked up and sewn in the same pairs for Border 2 after all trimming is completed.

   d. Cut continuous strip into nineteen 55" segments. Arrange vertically as desired. Stitch segments together. Press.

   e. Stitch 132 pairs of triangles into half-square triangle units for Border 2. Press.

2. BORDER 1: See Adding Borders, page 4.

3. BORDER 2: Stitch 34 triangle units together for each side of quilt. Adjust to fit quilt, if necessary. Stitch to quilt. See photo for direction of units. Stitch 32 triangle units together for top and bottom. Stitch to quilt. Press.

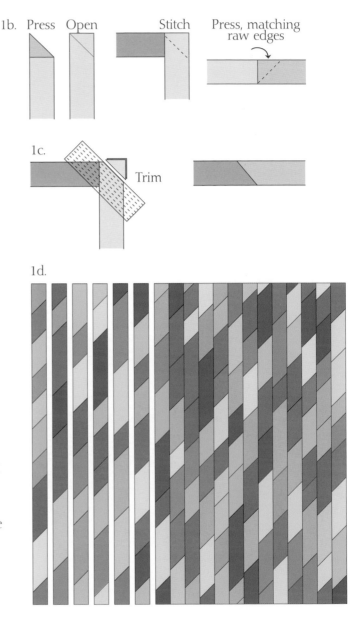

1b. Press Open   Stitch   Press, matching raw edges

1c.   Trim

1d.

1e.

4. BORDER 3: See Adding Borders, page 4.

5. LAYER, QUILT, & BIND: Piece backing horizontally to same size as batting. See Machine Quilting and Binding, page 5.

64 x 69"

YARDAGE Choose fabric with 42" usable width.

Quilt center,

Border 2	¼ yd each of 20 fabrics
	OR 1 roll of 20 strips 6½" wide
Border 1	⅓ yd
Border 3	1¾ yd
Binding	⅝ yd
Backing	4¼ yd
Batting	70 x 75"

CUTTING *Cut these strips from selvage to selvage.

Quilt center, Border 2	Cut from each fabric:
	*2 strips 3" wide
Border 1	*6 strips 1¼" wide
Border 3	*7-8 strips 6½" wide
Binding	*7 strips 2½" wide

DIRECTIONS Use ¼" seam allowance unless otherwise noted.

1. CENTER & BORDER 2:

   a. Using a rotary cutter, trim selvages from ends of strips with a careful 90° cut. Cut each strip, with a careful 90° cut, into 4 pieces: 6½", 8½", 10½", and 14½" long.

   b. Stitch all strips together end to end in random order using a diagonal seam: press 45° angle on end of strip to be placed on top each time, stitch on fold, and **do not trim** triangles at this time. Press all seam allowances in the same direction. See diagrams on page 16.

   c. Trim each seam with a rotary cutter and ruler, leaving ¼" seam allowance. Set pairs of triangles aside carefully so they can be picked up and sewn in the same pairs for Border 2 after all trimming is completed.

   d. Cut continuous strip into nineteen 53" segments. Arrange vertically as desired. Stitch segments together. Press.

   e. Stitch 122 pairs of triangles into half-square triangle units for Border 2. Press.

2. BORDER 1: See Adding Borders, page 4.

3. BORDER 2: Stitch 31 triangle units together for each side of quilt. Adjust to fit quilt, if necessary. Stitch to quilt. See diagram and photo for direction of seams. Stitch 30 triangle units together for top and bottom. Stitch to quilt. Press.

4. BORDER 3: See Adding Borders, page 4.

5. LAYER, QUILT, & BIND: Piece backing horizontally to same size as batting. See Machine Quilting and Binding, page 5.

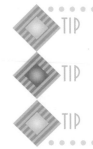

TIP

TIP

TIP

QUILTING IDEA
Quilt the vertical seams of the quilt center in the ditch, then add three parallel lines of quilting between the seams. Quilt the outer border with a lovely continuous-line feather design.

62 x 72"   10" Block

YARDAGE Choose fabric with 42" usable width.

Blocks	⅜ yd each of 10 fabrics, 5 of Color 1 & 5 of Color 2
	OR 1 roll of 20 strips 6½" wide
	Note: Roll must have 2 strips each of 10 fabrics, 5 fabrics of Color 1, and 5 fabrics of Color 2
Border 1	⅝ yd
Border 2	1 yd
Binding	⅝ yd
Backing	4 yd
Batting	68 x 78"

CUTTING *Cut these strips from selvage to selvage.

Blocks	Cut from each fabric:
	*4 strips 2½" wide
Border 1	*6 strips 2½" wide
Border 2	*7 strips 4½" wide
Binding	*7 strips 2½" wide

DIRECTIONS Use ¼" seam allowance unless otherwise noted.

1. BLOCKS: Cut all strips to the same length as the shortest one (not less than 42"). Make 4 identical strip sets using 5 strips of Color 1 and 4 identical strip sets using 5 strips of Color 2. Press. Cut each strip set into 4 blocks 10½".

2. ASSEMBLY: Arrange blocks in rows as shown, rotating every other block. Stitch into rows. Stitch rows together. Press.

3. BORDERS: See Adding Borders, page 4.

4. LAYER, QUILT, & BIND: Piece backing horizontally to same size as batting. See Machine Quilting and Binding, page 5.

1.
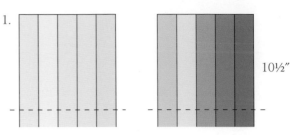

10½"

Make 4 strip sets & cut 4 blocks from each   Make 4 strip sets & cut 4 blocks from each

2.
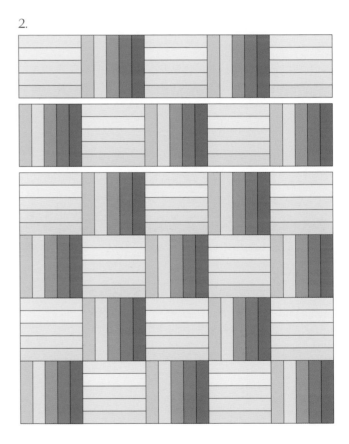

TIP

TIP

TIP

Two-color quilts are all-time favorites. Imagine this one in reds and whites or blacks and tans.

SONOMA VALLEY
SONOMA VALLEY

SONOMA VALLEY

62 x 72"   10" Block

YARDAGE Choose fabric with 42" usable width.

Blocks	¼ yd each of 20 fabrics, 5 fabrics each of 4 colors
	OR 1 roll of 20 strips 6½" wide,
	5 fabrics each of 4 colors
Border 1	⅝ yd
Border 2	1 yd
Binding	⅝ yd
Backing	4 yd
Batting	68 x 78"

CUTTING *Cut these strips from selvage to selvage.

Blocks	Cut from each fabric:
	*2 strips 2½" wide
Border 1	*6 strips 2½" wide
Border 2	*7 strips 4½" wide
Binding	*7 strips 2½" wide

DIRECTIONS Use ¼" seam allowance unless otherwise noted.

1. BLOCKS: Cut all strips to the same length as the shortest one (not less than 42"). Make 2 strip sets with each set of colors as shown. Press. Cut each strip set into 4 blocks 10½".

2. ASSEMBLY: Arrange blocks in rows as shown, rotating every other block. Stitch into rows. Stitch rows together. Press.

3. BORDERS: See Adding Borders, page 4.

4. LAYER, QUILT, & BIND: Piece backing horizontally to same size as batting. See Machine Quilting and Binding, page 5.

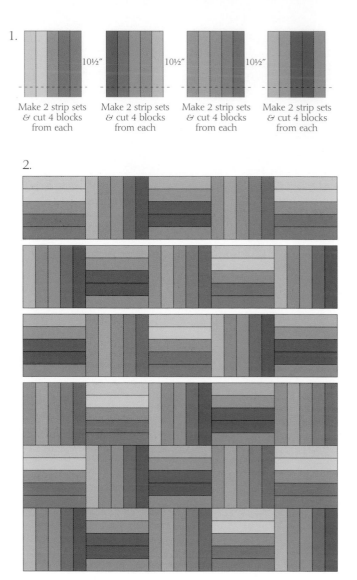

1.

Make 2 strip sets & cut 4 blocks from each   Make 2 strip sets & cut 4 blocks from each   Make 2 strip sets & cut 4 blocks from each   Make 2 strip sets & cut 4 blocks from each

2.

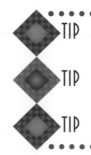

TIP

TIP

TIP

Nature can suggest a color scheme–the blue of the sky, the brown of the earth, and the green and purple of the vines. The theme is embellished by quilting grape clusters in alternate blocks and vines in the border.

IN THE PINK
IN THE PINK

52 x 68"

YARDAGE Choose fabric with 42" usable width.

Sashing, Border 2, applique	¼ yd each of 20 fabrics
	OR 1 roll of 20 strips 6½" wide
Applique background, Border 2	1⅓ yd
Additional applique fabrics	½ yd – vine
	⅙ yd each of 2 fabrics – leaves
	⅙ yd – flowers
	⅛ yd – flower centers
	⅛ yd – circles
Border 1	⅝ yd
Border 3	⅝ yd
Binding	⅝ yd
Backing	3½ yd
Batting	58 x 74"

CUTTING *Cut these strips from selvage to selvage.

Choose 16 fabrics for the sashing and Border 2, and use the other 4 for applique. See page 43 for using leftover strips in a pieced backing.

Group of 16 fabrics	sashing	*8 pieces 2 x 40½"
		*8 pieces 3 x 40½"
	Border 2	36 squares 2½"
Applique background, Border 2		*4 pieces 6½ x 40½"
		36 pieces 2½ x 4½"
Applique		See Step 1, patterns on p. 47
Border 1		*5-6 strips 2½" wide
Border 3		*6-7 strips 2½" wide
Binding		*7 strips 2½" wide

DIRECTIONS Use ¼" seam allowance unless otherwise noted.

1. APPLIQUE: Cut 8 bias strips 20" long and ¼-⅜" wide from vine fabric bonded with fusible web. Using photo and diagram as guides for placement, arrange 2 groupings of appliques on each background strip. Keep appliques at least ½" from edges. See Tip on page 12 for making leaves. See Fusible Web Applique, page 3.

2. ASSEMBLY: Arrange sashing and applique strips on floor, 2"-wide sashing strips on both long sides of each applique strip. Stitch into units shown. Stitch units together. Press.

3. BORDER 1: See Adding Borders, page 4. Stitch top and bottom borders to quilt first to avoid having to piece them.

1-2.

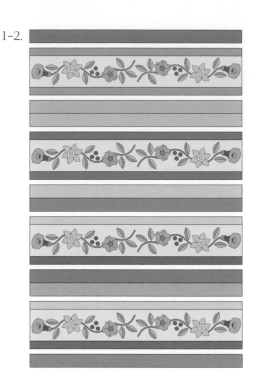

4.

4. BORDER 2: Stitch 10 background pieces and 10 pink squares together for each side border. Stitch 8 background pieces and 8 pink squares together for top and bottom. Stitch side borders to quilt oriented as shown. Repeat at top and bottom. Press.

5. BORDER 3: See Adding Borders, page 4. Stitch top and bottom borders to quilt first.

6. LAYER, QUILT, & BIND: Piece backing horizontally to same size as batting. See Machine Quilting and Binding, page 5.

TEDDY BEAR TIME
TEDDY BEAR TIME

52 x 68"

YARDAGE Choose fabric with 42" usable width.

Sashing, Border 2, panels	¼ yd each of 20 fabrics
	OR 1 roll of 20 strips 6½" wide
Muslin - panel foundations	⅞ yd
Border 1	⅝ yd
Border 2 background	½ yd
Border 3	⅝ yd
Binding	⅝ yd
Backing	3½ yd
Batting	58 x 74"

CUTTING *Cut these strips from selvage to selvage.

Group of 20 fabrics	sashing	8 pieces 2 x 40½"
		8 pieces 3 x 40½"
	Border 2	36 squares 2½"
	panels	See Step 1
Muslin		4 pieces 6½ x 40½"
Border 1		*5-6 strips 2½" wide
Border 2 background		36 pieces 2½ x 4½"
Border 3		*6-7 strips 2½" wide
Binding		*7 strips 2½" wide

DIRECTIONS Use ¼" seam allowance unless otherwise noted.

1. PANELS: From remaining pieces of the group of 20 fabrics, cut pieces 7" long by 2-4" wide, *a few at a time*. Place one colored strip at the center of a muslin foundation strip, right side up. Place another colored strip right side down on top of it, raw edges even. Stitch through all 3 layers ¼" from edge. Flip top piece over and press. Place subsequent strips at a slight angle; raw edges do not need to match. Stitch ¼" from raw edge of top piece. Trim edge of bottom colored piece even with edge of top colored piece, then flip top piece over and press. Be careful not to cut foundation. Repeat to end of foundation strip, then go back to center and work to other end of foundation strip. Trim to size of foundation. Make 4.

2. ASSEMBLY: Arrange sashing and panels on floor or design wall, 2"-wide sashing strips on both long sides of each applique strip. Stitch into units as shown. Stitch units together. Press.

3. BORDER 1: See Adding Borders, page 4. Stitch top and bottom borders to quilt first to avoid having to piece them.

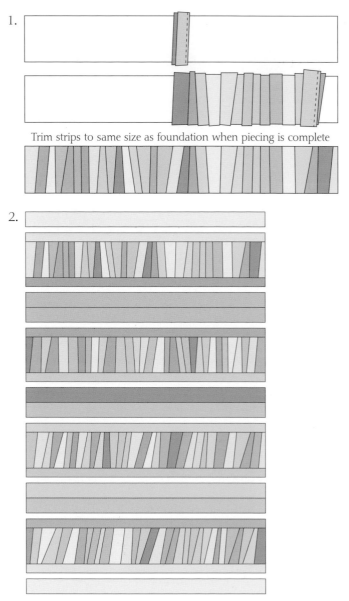

1.

Trim strips to same size as foundation when piecing is complete

2.

4. BORDER 2: Stitch 10 background rectangles and 10 squares together for each side border. Stitch 8 background rectangles and 8 squares together for top and bottom. Stitch side borders to quilt oriented as shown in diagram for Step 4 on page 24. Repeat at top and bottom. Press.

5. BORDER 3: See Adding Borders, page 4. Stitch top and bottom borders to quilt first.

6. LAYER, QUILT, & BIND: Piece backing horizontally to same size as batting. See Machine Quilting and Binding, page 5. Optional quilting pattern for sashing areas on page 48.

60 x 84"   12" Block

We suggest reading through the directions for this quilt before purchasing yardage. The cutting directions are very explicit because nearly every inch of the roll of 20 fabrics is used.

YARDAGE Choose fabric with 42" usable width.

Blocks	¼ yd each of 20 fabrics, blended light to dark
	OR 1 roll of 20 strips 6½" wide, blended light to dark
Centers	¼ yd each of 2 lights to coordinate with lights above
Border 1	½ yd
Border 2	1⅜ yd
Binding	⅔ yd
Backing	5⅜ yd
Batting	66 x 90"

CUTTING *Cut these strips from selvage to selvage.

Blocks	see Step 1
Centers	24 squares 3½"
Border 1	*7 strips 2" wide
Border 2	*7-8 strips 5" wide
Binding	*8 strips 2½" wide

DIRECTIONS Use ¼" seam allowance unless otherwise noted.

1. CUTTING FOR BLOCKS:

    a. Sort and label fabrics:

2 fabrics for Half-Round 1	4 fabrics for Half-Round 4
2 fabrics for Half-Round 2	4 fabrics for Half-Round 5
3 fabrics for Half-Round 3	5 fabrics for Half-Round 6

    b. Cut 3 strips 2" wide from each fabric.

    c. HALF-ROUND 1: Stack the 6 strips for Half-Round 1 and cut 24 pieces 3½" long (4 cuts), then cut 24 pieces 5" long (4 cuts). Label all pieces as Half-Round 1. *Reserve remaining pieces for Half-Round 2.* See diagram.

    d. HALF-ROUND 2: Stack the remaining pieces from Half-Round 1 and cut 6 pieces 6½" long (1 cut). Stack the 6 strips for Half-Round 2 together and cut 18 pieces 6½" long (3 cuts), then cut 24 pieces 5" long (4 cuts). Label all pieces as Half-Round 2.

    e. HALF-ROUND 3: Stack 5 strips and cut 25 pieces 8" long (5 cuts). Stack the remaining 4 strips and cut 24 pieces 6½" long (6 cuts). Label all pieces as Half-Round 3.

Continued on page 43.

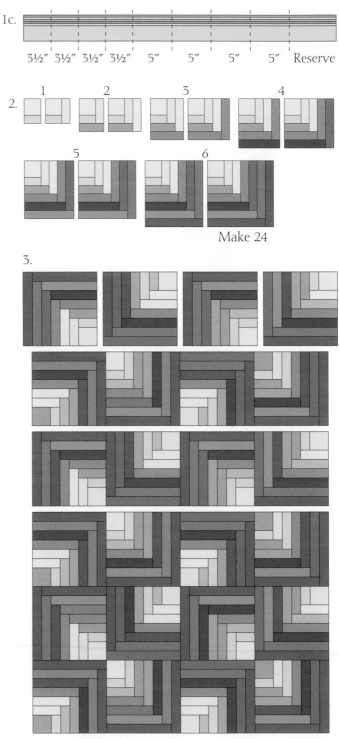

1c.

3½" 3½" 3½" 3½"   5"   5"   5"   5"   Reserve

2.   1   2   3   4   5   6   Make 24

3.

GRANNY'S SQUARES
GRANNY'S SQUARES

GRANNY'S SQUARES

60 x 72"   12" Block

Directions below are for a single-layer binding using 2" strips left over from blocks and applique. If a double-layer binding is desired, purchase ⅝ yd fabric and cut 7 strips 2½" wide.

YARDAGE Choose fabric with 42" usable width.

Block Half-Rounds 3-6, applique, binding	¼ yd each of 20 fabrics OR 1 roll of 20 strips 6½" wide
Centers, Block Half-Rounds 1-2	⅓ yd each of 5 fabrics
Applique	½ yd - vine
	⅛ yd ea of 2 fabrics - leaves
	⅛ yd ea of 3 fabrics - butterflies
Border	1½ yd
Backing	4 yd
Batting	66 x 78"

CUTTING *Cut these strips from selvage to selvage.

Block Half-Rounds 3-6, binding, applique	Cut from each fabric: *3 strips 2" wide
Centers, Half-Rounds 1-2	Cut from 1 fabric: 20 squares 3½"
	Cut from remaining 4 fabrics: *3-4 strips 2" wide
Applique	See Step 4, patterns on page 47
Border	*7 strips 6½" wide

DIRECTIONS Use ¼" seam allowance unless otherwise noted.

1. BLOCKS: See Step 2 diagrams on page 28. Stitch each strip to block, then trim end. Diagram at right. Press. Make 20.

2. ASSEMBLY: Arrange blocks in rows rotated as shown. Stitch into rows. Stitch rows together. Press.

3. BORDER: See Adding Borders, page 4.

4. APPLIQUE: Cut 8 bias strips 20" long and ¼-½" wide from vine fabric bonded with fusible web. See Tip box on page 12 for leaves. Cut pieces not listed in yardage chart from fabric left over after making blocks. Using photo and diagram as guides for placement, arrange appliques. See Fusible Web Applique, page 3.

5. LAYER, QUILT, & BIND: Piece backing horizontally to same size as batting. See Machine Quilting, page 5. For binding, cut leftover strips into 10-20" lengths. Stitch end to end to measure 275". Stitch to quilt in a single layer using a ⅜" seam allowance. Turn under raw edge on back before hand stitching. Also see Binding, page 5.

1.

Trim   Trim

2.

4.

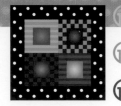

GLAD FOR PLAID
GLAD FOR PLAID

GLAD FOR PLAID

59x74"   8" Block

YARDAGE Choose fabric with 42" usable width.

Block centers,
   Border 2, binding   ¼ yd each of 20 fabrics
                           OR 1 roll of 20 strips 6½" wide
Block frames   1 yd each of 2 fabrics
Borders 1 & 3   1¾ yd
Backing   3⅞ yd
Batting   65x80"

CUTTING *Cut these strips from selvage to selvage.

Block centers, Border 2, binding   Cut from each fabric:
                                   1 square 5½"
                                   1 piece 2½ x 20"
                                   1 piece 3 x 13"
                                   5 squares 3"
Block frames   36 pieces 2x5½" of each fabric
                36 pieces 2x8½" of each fabric
Border 1   *3 strips 4¼" wide - sides
                *3 strips 3¾" wide - top & bottom
Border 3   *7 strips 4" wide

DIRECTIONS Use ¼" seam allowance unless otherwise noted.

1. BLOCKS:

   a. Sort 3x13" pieces into pairs. Make strip sets with each pair as shown. Press.

   b. Cut each strip set into 4 segments 3" wide.

   c. Make 2 four-patch blocks from each pair. Press.

   d. BLOCK A: Choose 18 four-patch blocks to frame. Using one frame fabric for all blocks, stitch short pieces to sides, then long pieces to top and bottom. Press.

   e. BLOCK B: Choose seventeen 5½" squares to frame. Repeat Step 1d with remaining frame fabric and 5½" squares.

2. ASSEMBLY: Place Blocks A and B alternately in rows, rotated as shown. Stitch blocks into rows. Stitch rows together. Press.

3. BORDER 1: See Adding Borders, page 4.

4. BORDER 2: Stitch 25 squares (3") together for each side of quilt. Stitch to quilt. Stitch 21 squares (3") together for top and bottom. Stitch to quilt. Press.

5. BORDER 3: See Adding Borders, page 4.

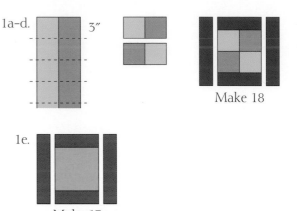

1a-d.   3"

Make 18

1e.

Make 17

2.

6. LAYER, QUILT, & BIND: Piece backing horizontally to same size as batting. See Machine Quilting, page 5. For binding, stitch 2½ x 20" pieces together end to end to measure 280". See Binding, page 5.

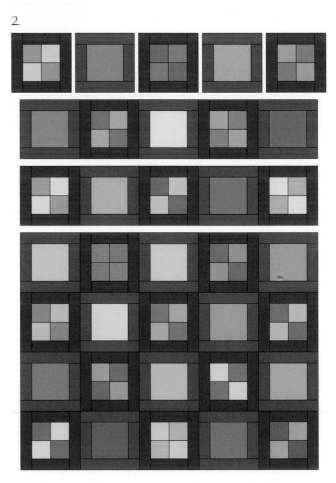

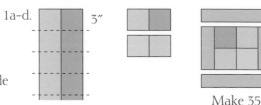

SPRING HAS SPRUNG
SPRING HAS SPRUNG

SPRING HAS SPRUNG

59x74"   8" Block

1a-d.   3"

Make 35

YARDAGE Choose fabric with 42" usable width.

Block centers, Border 2, binding	¼ yd each of 20 fabrics
	OR 1 roll of 20 strips 6½" wide
Block frames	⅜ yd each of 6 fabrics
Borders 1 & 3	1¾ yd
Backing	3⅞ yd
Batting	65x80"

2.

CUTTING *Cut these strips from selvage to selvage.

Block centers, Border 2, binding

Cut from each fabric:
*1 strip 2½" wide
2 pieces 3x13"
5 squares 3"

Block frames	12 pieces 2x5½" of each fabric
	12 pieces 2x8½" of each fabric
Border 1	*3 strips 4¼" wide – sides
	*3 strips 3¾" wide – top & bottom
Border 3	*7 strips 4" wide

DIRECTIONS Use ¼" seam allowance unless otherwise noted.

1. BLOCKS:

    a. Sort 3x13" pieces into pairs. Make strip sets with each pair as shown. Press.

    b. Cut each strip set into 4 segments 3" wide.

    c. Make 35 four-patch blocks as shown. Press.

    d. Stitch short frame pieces to sides, then long pieces to top and bottom. Press.

2. ASSEMBLY: Place blocks in rows, arranged and rotated as shown. Stitch blocks into rows. Stitch rows together. Press.

3. BORDER 1: See Adding Borders, page 4.

4. BORDER 2: Stitch 25 squares together for each side of quilt. Stitch to quilt. Stitch 21 squares together for top and bottom. Stitch to quilt. Press.

5. BORDER 3: See Adding Borders, page 4.

6. LAYER, QUILT, & BIND: Piece backing horizontally to same size as batting. See Machine Quilting, page 5. For binding, cut 2½" strips into thirds. Stitch end to end to measure 300". See Binding, page 5.

TIP

TIP

TIP

Choosing dark pastels in monotone prints for the frames perfectly sets off a roll of pastel multicolor prints.

BLACKBERRY BRANDY
BLACKBERRY BRANDY

50 x 67"   6½" Block

YARDAGE Choose fabric with 42" usable width.

Blocks ¼ yd each of 20 fabrics
OR 1 roll of 20 strips 6½" wide

Sashing, Border 2	2 yd
Border 1	½ yd
Binding	⅝ yd
Backing	3⅜ yd
Batting	56 x 73"

CUTTING *Cut these strips from selvage to selvage.

Blocks Cut from each of 5 fabrics:
*4 strips 1½" wide
Cut from each of 5 fabrics:
*3 strips 2" wide
Cut from each of 5 fabrics:
*2 strips 2½" wide
Cut from each of 5 fabrics:
*2 strips 3" wide

Sashing, Border 2 11 strips 3½" wide on lengthwise grain
Border 1 *6 strips 2" wide
Binding *7 strips 2½" wide

DIRECTIONS Use ¼" seam allowance unless otherwise noted.

1. BLOCKS: Cut all strips to the same length as the shortest one. Mixing fabrics and strip widths as desired, make 8 strip sets. Each strip set should have 6-8 strips and be 10-11" wide. Press. Cut four 7" squares "on point" from each strip set. Save leftovers for use in a pieced backing, if desired.

2. ASSEMBLY/SASHING: Stitch blocks into vertical rows as shown. Press carefully to avoid stretching all-bias edges. Take an average measurement of rows. Cut 5 sashing strips the average row length. Stitch sashing and block rows together, placing block rows next to feed-dog to help control bias edges. Press. Measure width of quilt and cut sashing for top and bottom. Stitch to quilt. Press.

3. BORDERS 1 & 2: See Adding Borders, page 4.

4. LAYER, QUILT, & BIND: Piece backing horizontally to same size as batting. See Machine Quilting and Binding, page 5.

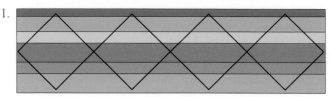

1.

Make 8 strip sets & cut four 7" squares "on point" from each

2.

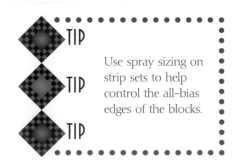

TIP
TIP
TIP

Use spray sizing on strip sets to help control the all-bias edges of the blocks.

AMISH STEPS

75 x 95"   5" Block

YARDAGE
Choose fabric with 42" usable width.

Blocks	¼ yd each of 20 fabrics
	OR 1 roll of 20 strips 6½" wide
Black	3⅝ yd
Border 1	⅝ yd
Border 2	1⅞ yd
Binding	¾ yd
Backing	6 yd
Batting	81 x 101"

CUTTING
*Cut these strips from selvage to selvage.

Blocks	Cut from each fabric:
	*2 strips 3" wide
Black	*40 strips 3" wide
Border 1	*8 strips 2" wide
Border 2	*8-9 strips 6½" wide
Binding	*9 strips 2½" wide

DIRECTIONS
Use ¼" seam allowance unless otherwise noted.

1. BLOCKS: Make 2 strip sets with each fabric and black. Press. Cut each strip set into 7 segments 5½" long. See Tip box below for organizing blocks to make ordered color arrangement like quilt in photo. Note: There will be extra blocks that can be used for a pieced backing. See page 43.

2. ASSEMBLY: Arrange blocks in rows as shown, rotating every other block. Use random color arrangement or ordered arrangement as shown in photo–see Tip box below. Stitch into rows. Stitch rows together. Press.

3. BORDERS 1 & 2: See Adding Borders, page 4.

4. LAYER, QUILT, & BIND: Piece backing vertically to same size as batting. See Machine Quilting and Binding, page 5.

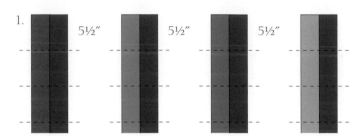

1.   5½"   5½"   5½"

Make 2 strip sets with each of the 20 fabrics paired with black

2.

TIP **TIP** **TIP**

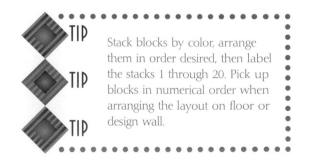

Stack blocks by color, arrange them in order desired, then label the stacks 1 through 20. Pick up blocks in numerical order when arranging the layout on floor or design wall.

CHRISTMAS RIBBONS
CHRISTMAS RIBBONS

56 x 68"   6" Block

YARDAGE Choose fabric with 42" usable width.

Reds & greens	¼ yd each of 20 fabrics, 10 each color
	OR 1 roll of 20 strips 6½" wide, 10 each color
Background	2¾ yd
Border 1	⅜ yd
Border 2	⅞ yd
Binding	⅝ yd
Backing	3¾ yd
Batting	62 x 74"

CUTTING *Cut these strips from selvage to selvage.

Reds & greens	Cut from each fabric:
	*2 strips 2" wide
Background	80 squares 6⅜" – cut in quarters diagonally
Border 1	*6 strips 1½" wide
Border 2	*6-7 strips 3½" wide
Binding	*7 strips 2½" wide

DIRECTIONS Use ¼" seam allowance unless otherwise noted.

1. BLOCKS:

    a. Cut 10 red and 10 green strips into 9½" segments for a total of 40 red and 40 green. Cut 10 red and 10 green strips into 4½" segments for a total of 80 red and 80 green. Sort these shorter segments into pairs.

    b. Make 40 as shown with long green and short red pieces. Make 40 with long red and short green pieces. Press.

    c. Using pattern on page 42, make a 6½" plastic template. Carefully transfer the blue markings to the template. Another method is to mark a 6½" square rotary ruler with ¼" masking tape. The goal is to trim the blocks exactly alike so the corners will meet perfectly.

    d. Trim the 80 blocks, matching the markings on the template or ruler with the seam lines.

2. ROW UNITS: Make 5 row units using diagram for placement of color and rotating blocks as shown. Press.

3. ASSEMBLY: Stitch row units together. Press.

4. BORDERS 1 & 2: See Adding Borders, page 4.

5. LAYER, QUILT, & BIND: Piece backing horizontally to same size as batting. See Machine Quilting and Binding, page 5. Quilting pattern for border on page 48.

1b.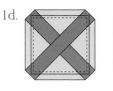

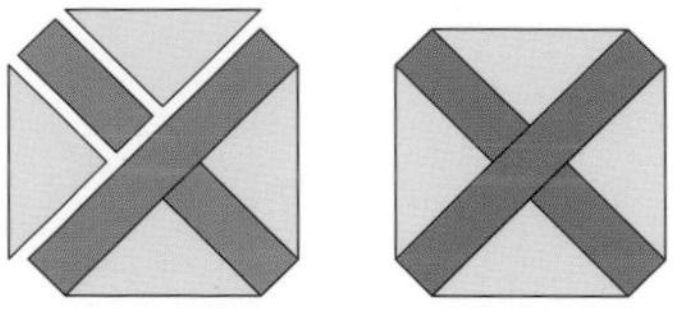

Make 40   Make 40

1d.

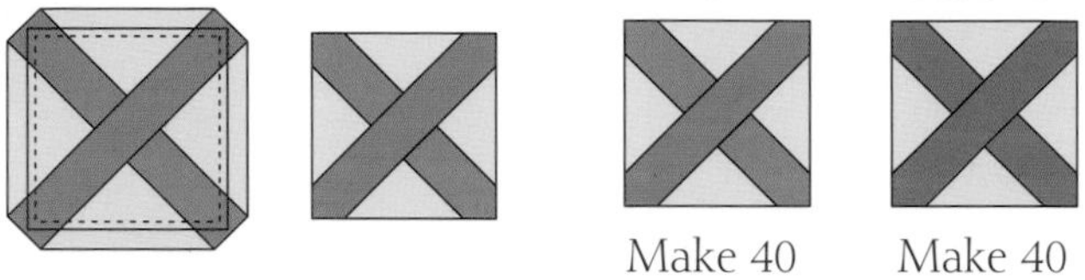

Block A   Block B

Make 40   Make 40

2. Row Unit – Make 5

3.

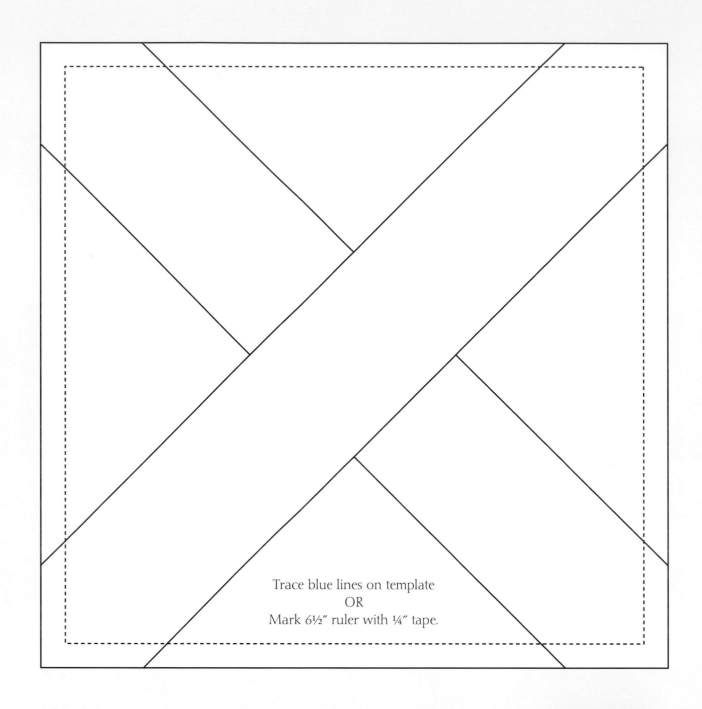

Trace blue lines on template
OR
Mark 6½″ ruler with ¼″ tape.

CHRISTMAS
RIBBONS

CHOCOLATE COVERED CHERRIES

Continued from page 28.

f. HALF-ROUND 4: Stack 5 strips and cut 25 pieces 8″ long (5 cuts). Stack the remaining 7 strips and cut 21 pieces 9½″ long (3 cuts). From the remaining pieces, cut 3 pieces 9½″ long. Label all pieces as Half-Round 4. *Reserve remaining pieces for Half-Round 5.*

g. HALF-ROUND 5: Stack 8 strips and cut 24 pieces 9½″ long (3 cuts), then cut 8 pieces 11″ long (1 cut). Stack the remaining 4 strips and cut 12 pieces 11″ long (3 cuts). Stack the remaining pieces from Half-Round 4 and cut 4 pieces 11″ long (1 cut). Label all pieces as Half-Round 5.

h. HALF-ROUND 6: Stack 8 strips and cut 24 pieces 11″ long (3 cuts). Save the remaining pieces. Stack the remaining 7 strips and cut 21 pieces 12½″ long (3 cuts). Using the remaining pieces from the first step in this paragraph, stitch 2 of the same fabric together 3 times. Press. Cut 3 pieces 12½″ long. Label all pieces as Half-Round 6.

2. BLOCKS: Make 24 blocks following diagrams. Press.

3. ASSEMBLY: Arrange blocks in rows rotated as shown. Stitch into rows. Stitch rows together. Press.

4. BORDERS: See Adding Borders, page 4.

5. LAYER, QUILT, & BIND: Piece backing vertically to same size as batting. See Machine Quilting and Binding, page 5.

IN THE PINK

To use the leftover pink strips for a pieced backing, cut them to approximately 17″ long and stitch them into a vertical row.

Stitch leftover blocks into vertical rows, rotating every other one, for a great pieced backing.

AMISH STEPS

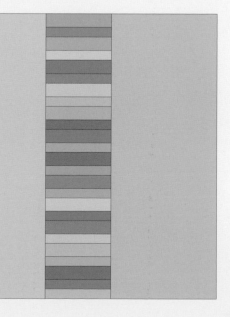

PERSIAN
BEAUTY

Make 4

Make 8

Make 24

Make 8

Make 8

Make 16

Make 16

Make 8

Make 8

Patterns are for fusible web applique,
reversed for tracing and no seam
allowances added. For placement., refer to
diagram and photo on pages 14 and 15.

44

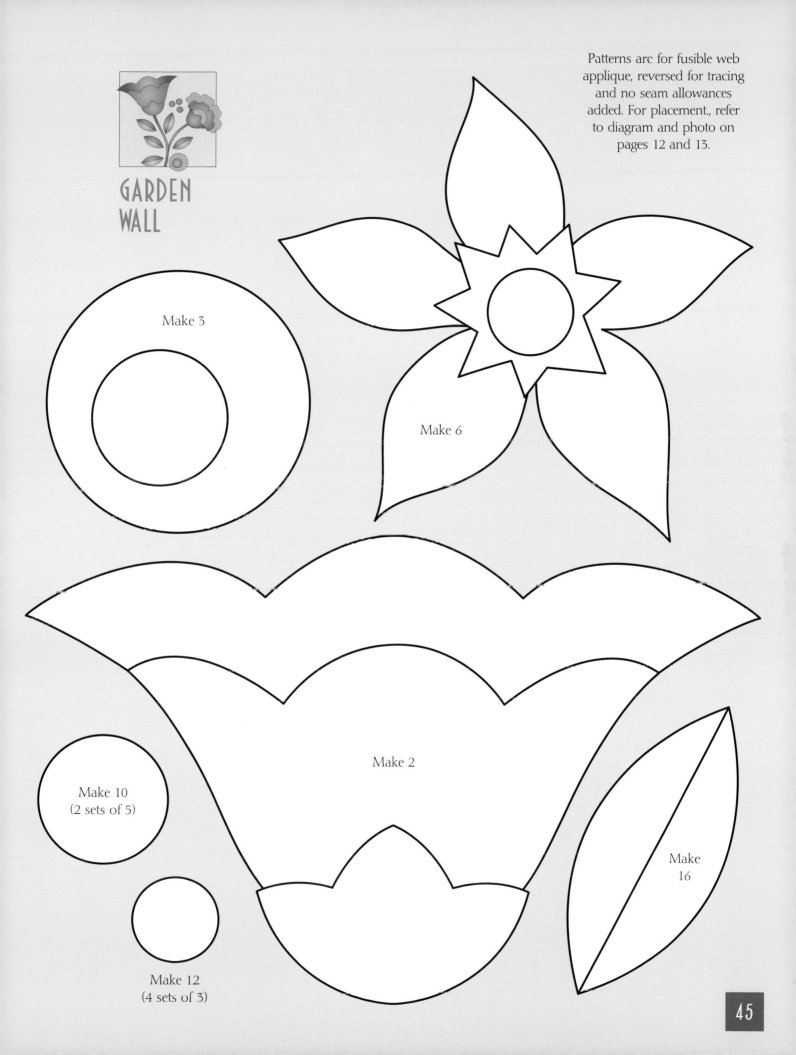

GARDEN WALL

Patterns arc for fusible web applique, reversed for tracing and no seam allowances added. For placement., refer to diagram and photo on pages 12 and 13.

Make 3

Make 6

Make 2

Make 10
(2 sets of 5)

Make 16

Make 12
(4 sets of 3)

GARDEN
WALL

Make 2

Make 2

Make 6

Make 5

Patterns are for fusible web applique, reversed for tracing and no seam allowances added. For placement, refer to diagram and photo on pages 12 and 13.

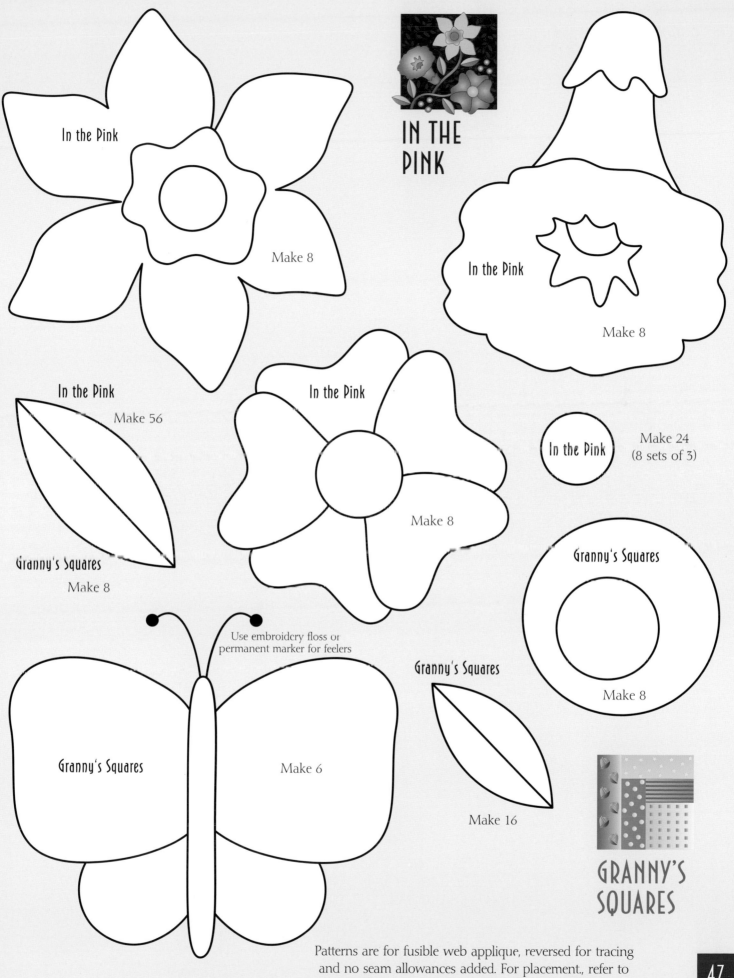

In the Pink

Make 8

IN THE PINK

In the Pink

Make 8

In the Pink

Make 56

In the Pink

Make 8

In the Pink   Make 24
(8 sets of 3)

Granny's Squares

Make 8

Granny's Squares

Make 8

Use embroidery floss or
permanent marker for feelers

Granny's Squares

Granny's Squares   Make 6

Make 16

GRANNY'S
SQUARES

Patterns are for fusible web applique, reversed for tracing
and no seam allowances added. For placement., refer to
diagrams and photos on pages 24-25 and 30-31.

TEDDY
BEAR
TIME

Use vine above and below a
row of bears (use the size given).

Enlarge vine 200% for top and
bottom sashing areas.

Match
repeats
here

Match
repeats
here

Match
repeats
here

CHRISTMAS
RIBBONS

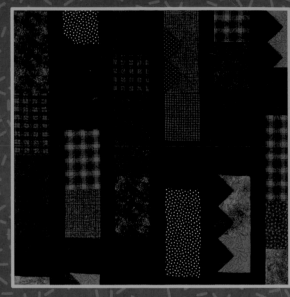

Study In Blue – Page 8

F abric lovers of the world—here is your chance to make more quilts! By using precut bundles of 6½" strips, now you can make any quilt in this book!

SUPER SIMPLE STRIPS INCLUDES

 18 fantastic quilts, 4 with specially designed appliqué

 Various suggestions for pieced backings—great way to utilize leftover fabrics!

Information for using rolls of precut strips, plus yardage requirements for buying off the bolt

Plenty of color inspiration and basic quilting tips and hints

ISBN 1880972522

☆ ☆ ☆ ☆ ☆
Possibilities®

. . . Fabric Designers for AvLyn, Inc, publishers of DreamSpinners®
patterns & I'll Teach Myself™ & Possibilities® books. . .

Home of Great American Quilt Factory, Inc.
8970 East Hampden Avenue • Denver, Colorado 80231
1-800-474-2665 • www.possibilitiesquilt.com

9 781880 972526

Gallery
of
American
Quilts

1860-1989   BOOK 2

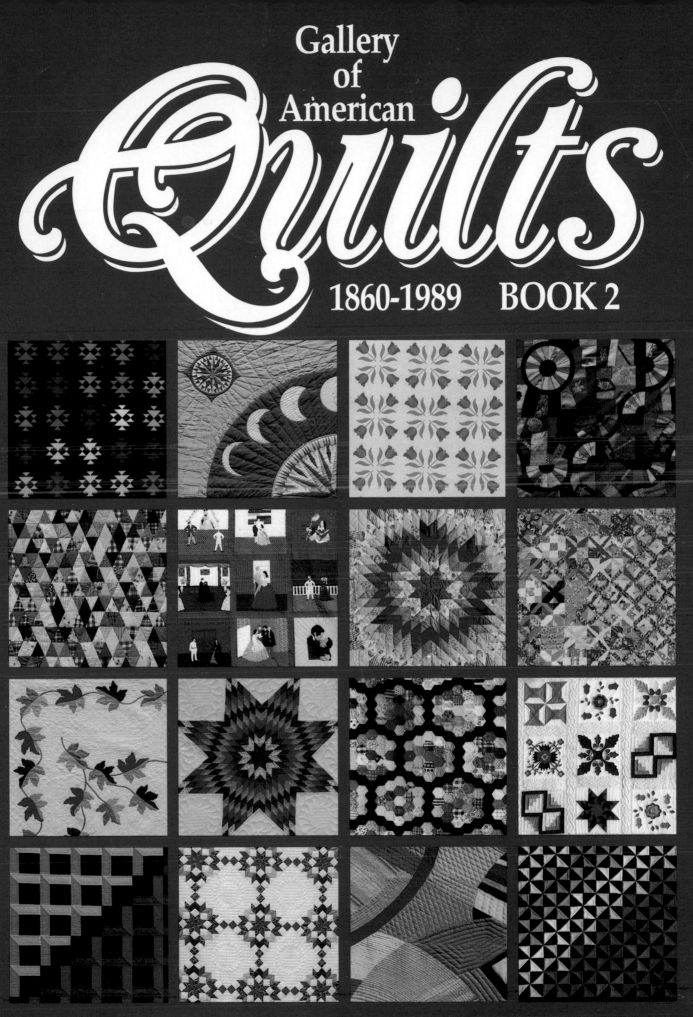

A collection of 875 quilts, and their values, presented by the American Quilter's Society